PEOPLE MOSTLY

The Amaryllis Press

PEOPLE MOSTLY

NEW YORK IN PHOTOGRAPHS 1900-1950

Benjamin Blom

Illustrations on preceding pages:

HALF-TITLE PAGE Mother and child at Ellis Island, c1910

TITLE PAGE Stranded subway crowd at the Kings Highway Station of the BMT Brighton Line. That time, the hour-long delay was caused by an explosion at the power plant, 1941. Irving Haberman

COPYRIGHT PAGE **right** Painting a flagpole, 1925 **left** Riggers, with the Woolworth Building in the background, c1935

Opposite Page, background photograph: Ichabod T. Williams' lumber yard, Eleventh Avenue between 25th and 26th Sts, c1900

Designed by Benjamin Blom. Printed by The Murray Printing Company, Westford, Massachusetts. Bound by Publishers' Book Bindery, Long Island City. Typesetting by Studio 305, New York.

Library of Congress Catalog Card Number: 83-071881
ISBN 0-943276-01-2

ACKNOWLEDGMENTS

Among those to whom I owe a particular debt of gratitude for the many valuable suggestions they made are Gary Chassman, Stanley Lewis, Joe Delgado, Newton Pincus, and Howard Batchelor.

Ed DeSantis made the mechanicals and acted as project coordinator; for his devotion, as much as for his great skills, I am most grateful.

Melissa Feldman executed my designs for the jacket, the preliminary pages, and the part-title pages, for which Concept Typographic Services set the display type. Sam and Ed Goldman of Publishers' Book Bindery went far beyond the call of duty (or business), as always, in giving advice essential to the making of books.

Many of those who generously contributed to the making of my previous book *NEW YORK* once again played a sometimes vital but always valuable role in the making of this book, dedicated to Willem and Henrietta, my parents, and to my daughter, Carol. Their spirit hovers over these pages.

CONTENTS

FOREWORD

People Mostly presents the people we love, the others we would love to trip up, and still others who make us cry, laugh, and run the whole gamut of human emotions. On the whole, allowing for the good and the bad, we're glad they were here; we want to see their faces, observe their gestures, understand their lives, and say thanks for having given us a world good enough to improve. Or try and improve.

The photographs have been selected (especially in such sections as *Seeing New Yorkers* and *Making It Work*) to provide a glimpse, to give a hint of a New York we might have experienced had we been there, day by day, and so felt the life, the pulse of the city, from the inside.

That inside view is often quite different that the impression gained by tourists who, like the caricatures of themselves, rush from one famous sight to the next, with no patience, no time, no desire to observe the seemingly mundane, the ordinary.

The past—New York 1900-1950 for example—can also be visited in that sort of manner, which incidentally has the advantage of allowing us to be ever so succinct, summarizing entire cities or historical periods in three words or less. But the price paid for ignoring the ordinary is considerable.

The ordinary is constantly with us, at times overwhelmingly so. When it is transformed to the extraordinary—by dint of insight and perception—we have broken through to the essence of things. The seemingly mundane, seen through receptive eyes, aided by the magic of the photographer's art, becomes the very source of amazement and ultimately deepest satisfaction.

Once we let in the ordinary, the mundane, even 1900-1950 New York ceases to be that unreal entity, the city of endless beauty, of perfection, of one magnificent landmark after another, icon piled upon icon, and we, historical tourists, satiated, exhausted, are bored. We need the imperfections, the sweat, the ordinary, to give things humanity.

And what could be more ordinary than watching two people (strangers?) in a street colloquium, so engrossed that they're oblivious to the presence of one of the world's most famous photographers, who is about to immortalize this pair—the Professor and the Vendor—in a wonderful photograph, reproduced on page 13, and signed "Anonimo", the Italian relative of "Anonymous".

Anonimo, artist supreme, heavily favored throughout this book, and (I confess) chosen over great artists with well-known names because their images, landmarks and masterpieces of photography, are seen again and again and again (and yes, some are also to be found in this book), whereas the most inspiring work of Anonimo is too often unjustly ignored. The extraordinary ordinary.

So there we have it, in the Professor and Vendor photograph, and in so many others in this book: New York, the city of human warmth, of interpersonal exchanges, of meaningful communications...And there it is, the diametrical opposite, also represented: New York, the city of loneliness, of isolation, of alienation, recorded in two photographs (pages 18 and 19) of scenes so ordinary that without the human element the photographs would be of little interest, merely documents of place and time.

These two images project these scenes onto another level in which prototypical New York symbols—the Hebrew-lettered sign, the El structure—are subordinated (in the case of the earlier photograph) to the human drama, that sense of isolation and alienation: the frozen figures and the cityscape a mere backdrop to heighten the dream-like, surrealistic dimension.

Thus we walk the city's streets, 1900-1950 (give or take a few years), and use the city as we see fit: we too want to gape at the famous sights, to relish the fantasy of the Chrysler's spire, the grandeur of Grand Central, and then turn to that bore of a Bronx street (page 23), there to discover kids playing, or on the facing page see an elderly woman in total isolation, an ominous shadow about to envelop her. And later, see women marching or flying (pages 33 and 34) to win options that should be theirs by birthright. New York, the city of ferment, of ideas, of conflicts, of diversity and variety; the city of multiple choices. Reflected, I hope you agree, in the photographs selected for this book.

In all this we are participants, even when merely spectators or readers of picture books. We decide where to go, what page to turn to, whether to run or to linger, and most important of all, how we want to see things: programmed, or as open-minded as reasonably possible.

Programmed would mean that we perceive this book's mission to be to tell us something about New York, its architecture and neighborhoods, ideally guiding us to things that are archetypically, prototypically, stereotypically (if not uniquely) New York.

Unique? Berenice Abbott's *Blossom Restaurant* is reproduced on page 51. Imagine that you're holding a photographic print, that you didn't recognize the artist or the photograph's provenance (from her *Changing New York*). Within that framework, I wouldn't have the foggiest notion whether Blossom is in Frisco, Boston, or Shartlesville, Pennsylvania, population 300.

The advantages of unprogramming ourselves, the benefits of not reading the captions until sufficient time has been spent looking at the photograph, are tremendous. That conscious ignorance of locale and time will encourage us to pay attention to the photograph's play of light and dark, the mysterious stranger emerging from that nether region, the person lurking behind that pole...every detail far more intriguing than using this image to document New York's architecture, neighborhoods, and such.

This book, like New York itself, is full of images that could be elsewhere, almost anywhere (why not Paris or Rome for the Professor?). One of the distinguishing qualities of New York is that it is so rich, so amazingly rich, that we can readily ignore the obvious—the Empire State Building—turn to the ordinary, and still feel that the sheer mass and variety of such things places us in New York. It is that wealth that allows us to use New York to transcend New York, to go beyond place and period.

In fact, if this book can be said to have any focus other than people, it is the negative focus of not seeking to document locale and period for their own sake, but to use such elements and scenes to evoke feelings.

For example, despite the relatively large group of Ellis Island photographs (as a pre-World War Two Dutch import, I'm hardly unbiased; in this book, immigrants are "in"), there's barely a hint of what Ellis Island looked like, inside or outside. What does come across, as we move from page 60 to page 68, is what it may have felt like to be poor, to pick up your roots, take the arduous ocean journey, and then face the nurses and guards (speaking a foreign language) who at

the flip of the hand could propel you into the rejected category, with its frighteningly high suicide rate. Or send millions New York-bound, ticketed, up the gangplank and then down, to step into Manhattan, head up high, smiling and full of hope, and take the first walk in its streets.

The objective is to elicit feelings, the means are photographs, some of which are fragments,

Illustration number 66. For detail, see page 62.

closeups, blowups, or images sequenced in photographic essays (for example, on women). The intent is to get the "I" involved; the me, the myself...and thus to encourage that *I* to propel itself into scenes as much as reasonably possible.

In that respect *People Mostly* echoes *New York: Photographs 1850-1950*, of which this is the extensively reworked concise edition, re-arranged and re-designed, with many additional photographs to strengthen the people-oriented sections. Most of that earlier volume's more specialized and purely architectural images have been eliminated. However, architecture (and photographs of things architectural) provides the perfect rationale for including photographs as wondrous as Bill Thomas' aerial photograph (page 148) of the swastika-emblazoned Hindenburg floating gently over a peaceful New York. Or is it sneaking up, and is this photograph a metaphor for liberty threatened by things that initially look so innocent, even so pleasant and attractive?

Finally, candor forces me to admit that this book contains a lie; a quite deliberate, blatant lie. I'll lead up to this sensitive matter gingerly. It is a well-known fact that ever since the invention of photography there has been hanky-panky; photographs and photographers have lied.

To an already snow-laden scene, snowflakes have been added, descending in such a mechanically perfect pattern that it's clear the flakes are fakes. In other instances, dramatic images may have been posed (Jacob Riis' *Street*

Arabs comes to mind), and seemingly posed images may have been spontaneous. How else can we explain the madcap quality of the Byron studio's wedding photograph on page 27? I'm reasonably certain no member of that wedding party wanted or *bought* that collective portrait—that dummy-like posture of the man at stage left, the challenging look of the woman at lower center; with one exception, no two persons look at each other, or do the other routine thing, eyes on the camera—the whole scene being a study in disorganization. If it is organized disorganization, it is further proof of the genius of the Byron studio; if not, it is a tribute to their delicious sense of humor: they preserved the photographic plate, made a wonderful print, and thus enriched this book.

To this bit of hocus-pocus and innocent merriment, I have added a gross example of deceit—if photographers can get away with it, why not picture editors?—in connection with the Triangle Shirtwaist fire (pages 90-93), a horror that has far more to do with avarice, officially sanctioned negligence, cover-up, and injustice, than with the accidental.

I confess: the young woman with a gas pipe in front of her throat, first seen on page 89, then on page 91, did not have the remotest connection with that disaster. She probably never set a foot in that factory. Be that as it may, it was certainly not she who was consumed by that fire, nor was it her body that broke the pavement eight stories below, nor was it she whose remains were placed in that coffin. All that sequencing, all those clear inferences are lies. Utter nonsense. A deception. A device. A gimmick to avoid meaningless numbers (numbers beyond comprehesion). But a means. A means to see One, a closeup, to look her straight in the eyes, and to particularize the horror of a life wasted and wantonly destroyed.

There is no more truth to this device than there is to the belief that Richard II spoke the words attributed to him by Shakespeare, or that the spirit of the Dodgers hovers over Brooklyn still, or that you know the waiter, wiping his brow and looking at his tip, seen on page 81.

In fact, if truth be known, New York 1900-1950 is alive. The past is present. Photographs prove it. Just look. Listen to their soul, guided by the I.

Fall, 1983   Benjamin Blom

Postscript:

In *The Measurement Of Man* (1981, Norton) Stephen Jay Gould cites an example of photographic hocus-pocus and hanky-panky that is anything but innocent or benign, and had a devastating effect upon immigration to this country during the first half of the century. Photographic fakery was only one of the means used to malign and unjustly exclude would-be immigrants on the basis of racial and ethnic background.

H.H.Goddard, a prominent scientist, believed that human intelligence is innate and biologically determined; that environment and society play a very small role indeed. He also believed, based upon observations made at Ellis Island, that fully 50% of Italian, Jewish, Slavic, and other immigrants (but assuredly not Anglo-Saxons and Nordics) were feeble-minded and morons, and so would be their offsprings.

These morons, said Goddard, can be spotted by facial features. He wrote *The Kallikak Family* (1912, Macmillan), mustering a mass of purported evidence, replete with photographs of alleged morons; a handy field guide to identification. Goddard failed to mention however, that these photographs had been heavily retouched in order to support his claim. This fakery was hardly innocent: Goddard's theories were used in the 1920's as a rationale to revise our immigration laws, all on the pretext that the changes would keep out the alleged genetically inferior. Consequently, hundreds of thousands of people attempting to come to these shores were arbitrarily and capriciously excluded; people who otherwise might well have contributed to our city's wealth, or have been saved from the holocaust.

PHOTOGRAPH SOURCES

Unless another source is cited below, the photographs in this book are taken from the publisher's collection. For the most part, that collection was gathered from private and other sources by Cityana Gallery, now closed. Over the course of several decades, photographs from the Library of Congress were also absorbed into these holdings.

Alexander Alland, Sr.: 123, 153, 165, 168

Archives of the Cathedral of St. John the Divine: 150

Brown Brothers: 5, 8, 9, 34, 36, 44, 49, 56, 61, 65, 68, 71, 72, 73, 74, 75, 85, 91, 96, 98, 99, 100, 102, 103, 104, 105, 107, 109, 135, 139, 149, 152, 157

Columbia University, Avery Architectural Library: 125, 142

Culver Picture Services: half-title page, title page, copyright page, 6, 7, 17, 50, 51, 58, 59, 62, 66, 67, 69, 70, 76, 77, 82, 101, 106, 111, 113, 119, 126, 127, 134, 143, 148, 151, 160, 161, 172, 173

Janet Lehr: 171

The Metropolitan Museum of Art: 110

The Museum of Modern Art: 87

The Museum of the City of New York: 11, 12, 18, 19, 20, 22, 23, 24, 25, 26, 35, 37, 38, 40, 60, 83, 88, 89, 90, 92, 93, 118, 154, 166

New York City, Department of Ports and Terminals: 169

The New York Historical Society: 2, 4, 28, 29, 30, 31, 32, 115, 116, 117, 132

Welcome to New York City: 41, 55, 94, 95, 97

Wide World Photo: 112

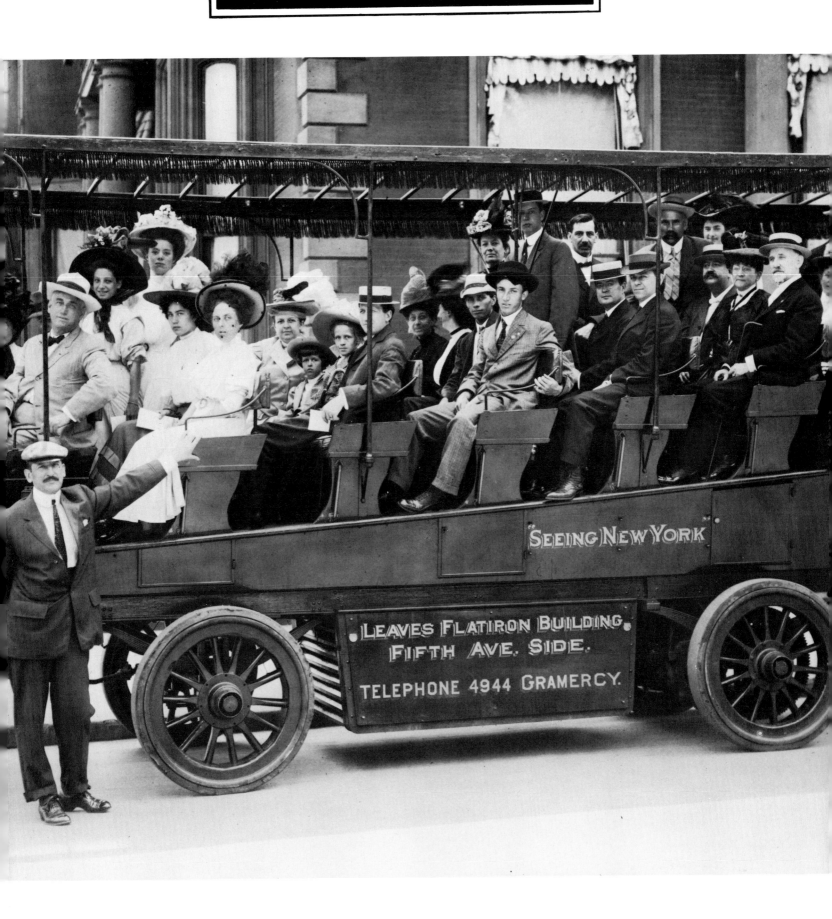

SEEING NEW YORK

LEAVES FLATIRON BUILDING
FIFTH AVE. SIDE.

TELEPHONE 4944 GRAMERCY.

2

Part title illustration (preceding page)
[1] Tourists about to see New York, c1912

The Difference a Place Makes
[2] Cab stand at Madison Square (also known
as Madison Park or Madison Square Park),
23rd to 26th Sts, between Fifth and Madison
Avenues, looking south toward Fifth Avenue,
c1900. Byron studio [3] Dancing on the deck
of a Hudson River excursion boat, c1900

4

Street Encounters [4] Passing them by at Fifth Avenue and 58th St, c1925. Irving Browning [5] A colloquy (*The Professor and the Vendor*) c1915

5

6

**Displaying the Fineries, or the
Street as Theatre** [6] Broadway and
9th St, 1905 [7] Harlem, 1940s

7

8

Mirth in the Streets [8] Boys on South St, below the Manhattan Bridge pier, c1910 [9] On Monroe St, south of the Manhattan Bridge, c1910

9

10

The Obverse Side [10] Under the El, Bowery, 1903. H.C. White [11] Columbus Avenue and 72nd St station of the El, 1938. Berenice Abbott

11

12

Inside, Outside [12] Improvised
dart game in Harlem, late 1930s.
Roy Perry [13] Apartment building
on Eagle Avenue in the Bronx, 1941

MESSENGER CONSTRUCTION
EAGLE AVE 156 ST TO WESTCHESTER AVE

14

The End is the Beginning, or Life as Metaphor [14] Villa Avenue looking north toward Van Cortlandt Avenue, the Bronx, 1941 [15] Villa Avenue looking north from above Bedford Park Boulevard, 1941

15

16

A Matter of Class [16] Men on
the steps of an unidentified
Astoria, Queens institution, c1900
[17] Fumigating clothes, Bowery,
1941. Norman Kaplan

17

18

Eyes on One, Eyes on None
[18] Bridesmaids' dinner given by
Mrs. Eben Wright at her 10 West
53rd St residence, 1905. Byron studio
[19] Wedding party (Harper), 1899.
Disorganized organization, or vice
versa. Byron studio

19

21

Window Dressings and Interiors
[20] A Broadway florist placed scantily dressed young women on a pedestal in his window to attract customers, a device adapted from the "living picture" models that were the vogue of music halls, 1901. Byron studio
[21] A woman and her children in a lower East Side dwelling, c1910. Jessie Tarbox Beals

22

A Matter of Class and Gender
[22] Young woman in her lodging,
1908. Byron studio [23] Two bache-
lors in theirs, one a Mr. Fox, tailor,
1904. Byron studio

23

24

25

Movers and Shakers [24-26] Dr. Latson's Method of Women's Self Defense, 1906. Byron studio [27] Woman suffrage rally at Union Square, 1916 [28] Women lawyers (*continued*)

27

28

in a suffrage parade, with Flatiron Building in the background, 1913
[29] Women marching at Fifth Avenue and 42nd St. Looking north with
Temple Emanu-El at right, 1912

30

Flying [31] Woman suffrage group at Midland Beach airstrip, Staten Island, December 2, 1916. Mrs Richberg Hornsby (at the controls) about to fly over President Wilson's yacht to drop petitions supporting the Susan B. Anthony Amendment. Gertrude A. Brugman [30] Detail [32] Suffragist Mrs. Richberg Hornsby. Gertrude A. Brugman

31

Women, at City Hall and in Harlem [33] The Liberty Loan Choir performs on the steps of City Hall in support of the Third Liberty Loan, April 1918, Bishop William Wilkinson conducting [34] Three women waiting in the Harlem office of the *Crisis* magazine, c1915

35

Two Realities [35] Jitterbugging in a Harlem ballroom, 1939. Sid Grossman [36] Night of the riot, Lenox Avenue at 135th St, August 3, 1943

508
OLIFF BROS.
LOAN OFFIC
APARTMENTS
FOR RENT
3·4·5 ROOMS
Inq. Supt. At 504 Apt. 14
AMOND
508

37

Night and Day [37] Harlem street-
corner meeting, early 1940s
[38] Union Square as a forum for
debates, mostly political, late 1940s.
Arnold Eagle

38

Women Acclaimed [39] Parade for
Gertrude Ederle, first woman to swim the
English Channel, on Broadway above St. Paul's
Chapel, August 27, 1926 [40] Amelia Earhart
at her reception on the steps of City Hall, with
Mayor Jimmy Walker about to present her
with a medal, June 1932

On to the Ocean [41] Background image: Aerial photograph of Coney Island, 1940s [42] Jumping the rope, 1891 [43] Holding the rope, 1891. Underwood & Underwood [44] Their bathing suits did get wet, 1895 [45 & 46] Fun and games, c1900 [47] Waiting in line for the Municipal Baths, c1900. William Zerbe

48

On to the Waterways
[48] Washington Bridge and the
High Bridge looking south down the
Harlem River during the Bangs Cup
Regatta, 1926. Saratoga's winning
crew and, at right, the second-place
team from Poughkeepsie [49] Swimming in the Hudson River, c1910

49

Those Glorious Days [50] Celebrating the Brooklyn Dodgers' pennant victory over the St. Louis Cardinals in Fitzgerald's Bar on Atlantic Avenue, 1941 [51] Dodgers fan at Ebbets Field, 1947. Peter Killian

51

52

[52] 204th St west of Villa Avenue,
the Bronx [53] Blossom Restaurant,
103 Bowery, 1935. Berenice Abbott

53

54

[54] Women on Fifth Avenue, near 50th St, 1936. Underwood & Underwood [55] Group photograph taken at the Garden Restaurant, Seventh Avenue and 50th St, 1915. White

THE GARDEN RESTAURANT 50 ST & 7 AVE

55

56

Lost in the Crowd [56] Albert Einstein on the steps of City Hall with Mayor Hyland, April 5, 1921. Not a single person is paying attention to the Professor

IMMIGRANTS ALL

58

59

Part title illustration (preceding page)
[57] Italians arriving on the S.S. *Patricia*,
1906. Edwin Levick

60

By Boat, By Plane [58] New York-bound immigrants on the steerage deck of the S.S. *Pennland*, 1893. Byron studio [59] Puerto Ricans landing at Idlewild (now Kennedy), Airport, 1947 [60] Immigrants arriving at Ellis Island, c1910

61

The Confident Ones [61] Jewish
refugees from Nazi Germany, 1930s
[62] Irish, c1920

64

[63] Italians aboard the S.S.
Madonna, 1920s [64] Caribbean,
1908

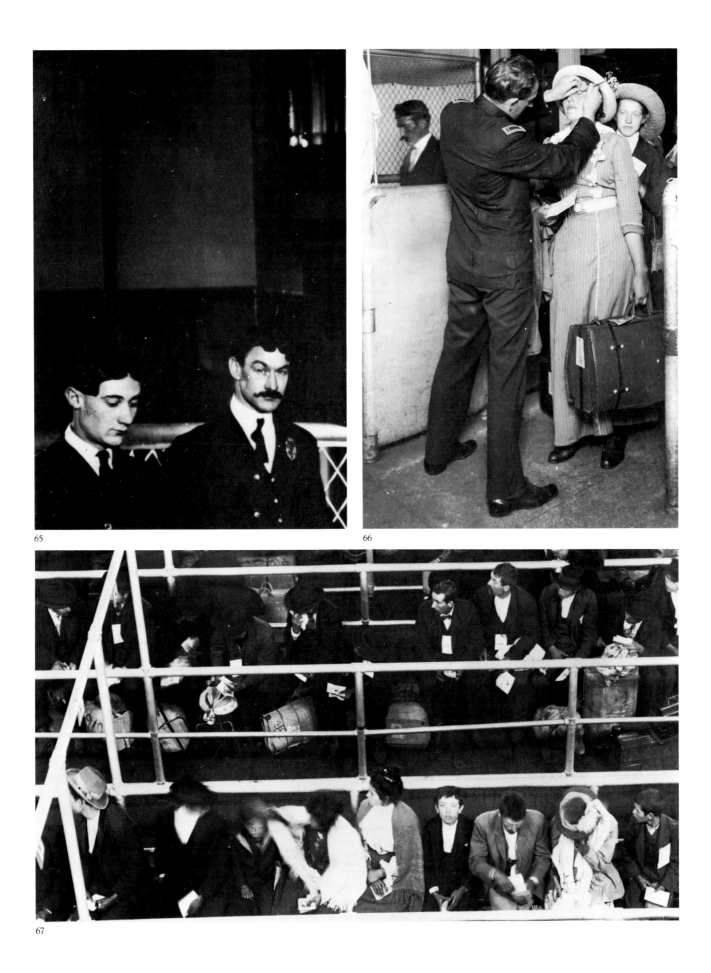

65

66

67

Ellis Island (photographs from the turn of the century) [65] Eye examination [66] U.S. Immigration Service officers [67] Waiting [68] Young peasant woman undergoing a physical examination

68

70

Together and Apart at Ellis Island [70] Women and children, c1900 [71] Men, c1900 [69 & 72] Details

71

72

Packed, Labeled, and Ready to Depart
[73 & 75] Italians, c1900
[74] Mid-European women, c1920

73

74

Manhattan-Bound [76] Italian immigrants, c1905

Manhattan Explored [77] Immigrant family taking a stroll on the lower East Side, c1910

79

Streets and Markets of Lower Manhattan [79] Looking north
along Mulberry St from above Baxter St, 1904. Detroit Publishing
Company [80] Northeast corner of Hester and Essex Sts, looking
east along Hester St, c1895. Langill and Bodfish [78 & 81] Details

80

81

82

[82] Harlem citizenship class for Italian
women, 1939. Roy Perry [83] Elderly
Jewish women learning to write English. Grand Street Settlement, c1939.
Roy Perry

83

84

End and Beginning [84] Puerto Rican American family in their Manhattan home, 1947

86

Part title illustration (preceding page)
[85] Newspaper vendor at work, early 1930s

[86] New York architects at the Beaux Arts Ball (1931), each
crowned with his own building. William Van Alen of the Chrysler
Building at center. From left to right: A. Stewart Walker of the 57th
St Fuller Building; Leonard Schultze of the Waldorf-Astoria; Ely
Jacques Kahn of the Squibb Building; Ralph Walker of One Wall St;
D.E. Ward of the Metropolitan Life Tower; and J.H. Freedlander of
the Museum of the City of New York [87] Construction of the
Triborough Bridge, 1936

87

88

[88] Class at the National Fruit and
Flower Guild, 247 Spring St, 1906.
Byron studio [89] Demonstration at
the Aeolian Company, 27 West 42nd
St, 1906. Byron studio

89

90

[90] The billiard players. Mrs. Frances
Hoppe and her son "Willie", 1900.
Byron studio [91] Waiter at the
Biltmore Hotel Cascade Ballroom,
early 1920s

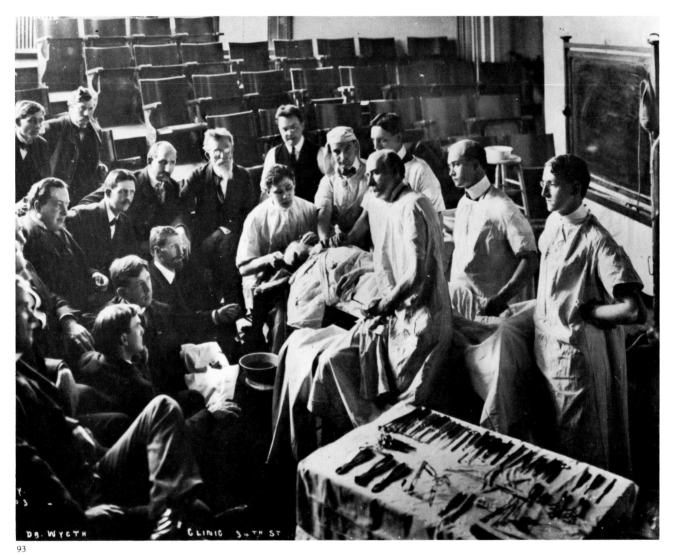

93

[92] Nurses descending the stairs,
St. Luke's Hospital, 1899. Byron
studio [93] Dr. John Allen Wyeth
lecturing before surgery at the New
York Polyclinic Medical School and
Hospital, 1902. Byron studio

94

Work is Work is Work
[94] Tex Austin's Rodeo at Yankee
Stadium, c1920 [95] Streetcar repair
crew in front of an unidentified
maintenance building, c1910

95

96

Clothing
[96] Selling a coat on the lower East
Side, c1910 [97] Selling lingerie in a
hotel ballroom, c1930

97

98

Clothing
[98 & 99] Unidentified New York
clothing factories, c1910

99

100

101

Clothing
[100 & 101] The Triangle Shirtwaist Company fire
(March 5, 1911), in which more than 145 people, almost
all young women, were killed [102] Many jumped to
their death [103] Unidentified garment worker, detail of
plate number 97

102

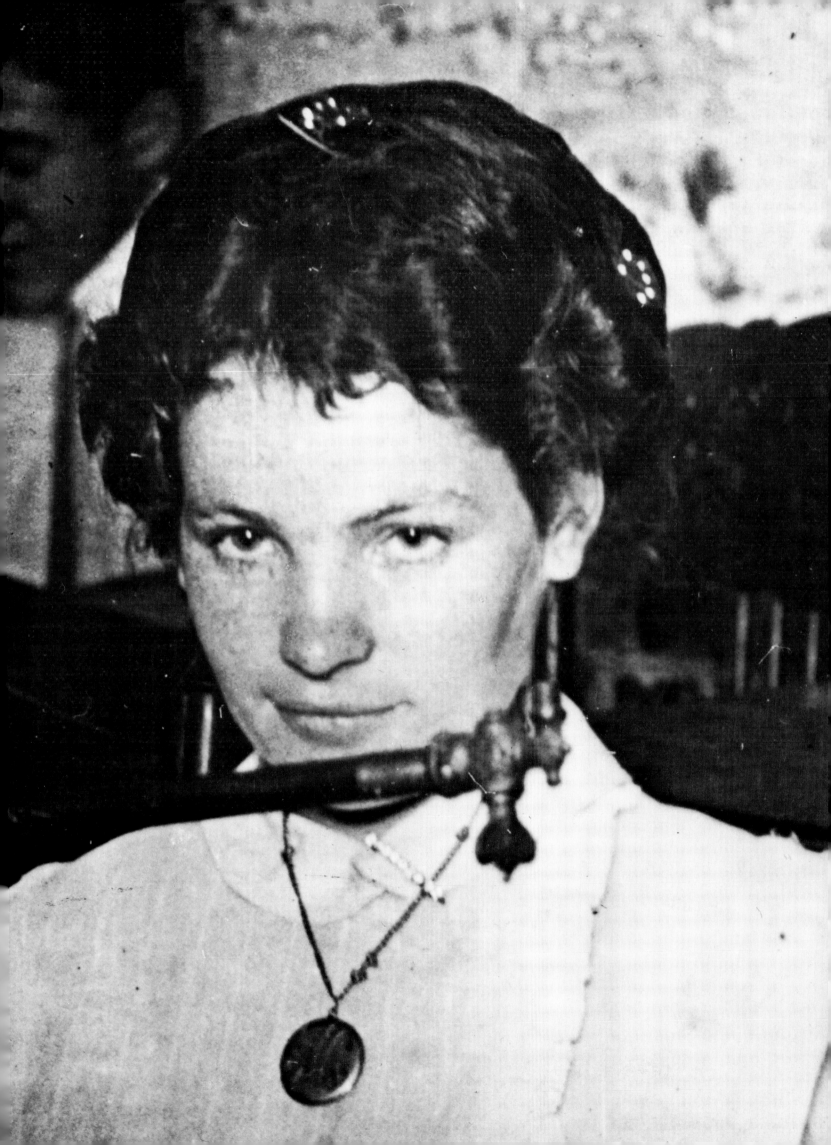

104

Clothing
[104] The Triangle fire. Identifying bodies in the morgue, 1911
[105] Unidentified garment workers demonstrating, 1911

105

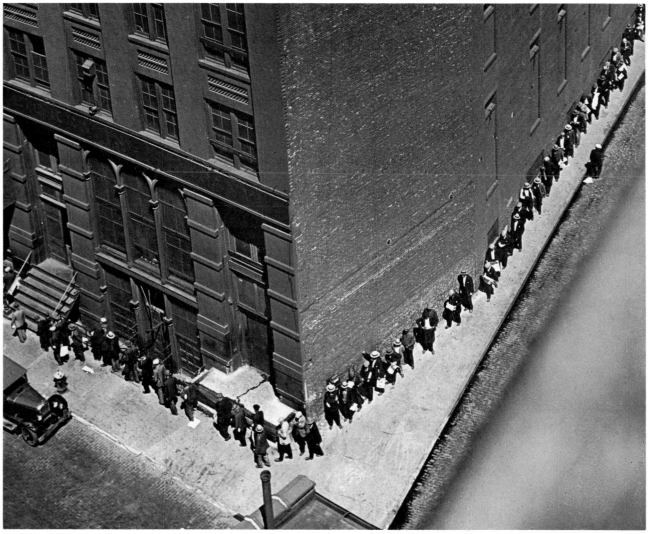

106

[106] Line of unemployed
men on Water St, 1932
[107] Handing out bread,
1930s

107

108

[108] Guards protecting the Williams-
burg Sugar Plant against strikers,
1910 [109] Garment workers' strike,
1912

109

110

Building the City
[110] Construction of the East Side
Highway, early 1930s

112

Part title illustration (preceding page)
[111] Photographer climbing toward a
Brooklyn Bridge tower, looking north, c1905

[112] Traders on the floor of the New York
Stock Exchange, late 1940s [113] Wall St,
looking west from William St, c1900

[114] The Equitable Building, east side of Broadway between Pine and Cedar Sts. The interior of the first building, erected in 1872 (enlarged in 1887 and gutted by fire in 1912), c1906. Detroit Publishing Company

[115] Cities Service Building (also known as Sixty Wall Tower) at 70 Pine St, looking northeast with the Brooklyn and Manhattan Bridges at left, c1932. Browning studio

116

[116] South St looking north from Old Slip, with the ramp of the Brooklyn Bridge in background, early 1890s [117] East River swimming scene at Pier 23, with Fulton Fish Market at right, 1892

117

118

[118] St. Paul's Chapel, at the corner
of Broadway and Vesey St, c1900.
Edwin Levick [119] Lower
Manhattan, looking south from the
lower West Side, with the Woolworth
and Singer towers dominating the
skyline, c1916. Jackson & Whitman

119

120

Woolworth Building [120] Tower
and Observatory, looking north toward Varick St (at top left). Photograph probably taken from a dirigible,
c1920 [121] Spire peeking above
the clouds, June 4, 1927. Fairchild
Aerial Surveys

121

122

[122] Jefferson Market Courthouse
(now Library) fronting Sixth Avenue.
Looking west along 10th St, 1906.
Detroit Publishing Company
[123] Washington Square art show,
with the Washington Arch and One
Fifth Avenue in the background, 1938.
Alexander Alland, Sr.

123

124

Pennsylvania Station [124] The Concourse, 1912 [125] The Concourse and tracks under construction, 1909. L.H. Dreyer. Both photographs depict the station designed by McKim, Mead and White, and wantonly destroyed in the 1960s

126

Empire State Building
[126] Aerial view, 1936. Fairchild
Aerial Surveys [127] The Observa-
tion Deck, 1940s

127

128

129

[128] Christmas window display, R.H. Macy's, 1910
[129] Corner of 34th St and Broadway. At left, 34th St;
in the center, Macy's; at right, the arcaded *New York
Herald* Building, and, to its left, the Times Tower, 1907
[130] Construction of Rockefeller Center's Radio City,
April 1932. Looking south toward the Empire State
Building, with Sixth Avenue below

130

131

Chrysler Building [131] Construction worker on the Empire State Building, with the Chrysler Building (also in constuction) in the background, 1930 [132] Looking northeast, 1930. Browning studio

133

Grand Central Terminal
[133] Main concourse, 1940. John
Collier [134] Main concourse, c1925.
Edwin Levick

136

Times Square [135] VE Day cele-
bration, May 8, 1945. Looking south
from 45th St [136] Watching news
bulletins on the electric signboard on
the Times Tower, early 1940s.
Marjory Collins

138

[138] Aerial photograph. Looking
south from about 58th St. The New
York Central Building (now the
Helmsley Building) straddles Park
Avenue, casting a shadow north to
the Waldorf-Astoria Hotel; the
Rockefeller Center complex at ex-
treme right, 1936. William Thomas
[137] Detail

140

[139] Fifth Avenue near 48th St. Charles Scribner's Sons, Saks Fifth
Avenue, and St. Patrick's Cathedral. Late 1920's [140] Looking
northeast from approximately 45th St and Sixth Avenue towards St.
Patrick's Cathedral, illuminated to mark the return of Cardinal Farley
from Rome, 1911 (Few photographs more dramatically demonstrate
the changed and changing city)

141

[141] Special illumination of the RCA Building. Looking west from Fifth Avenue, January, 1935. Louis Werner [142] Lee Lawrie's sculpture *Atlas* before casting and installation in the forecourt of Rockefeller Center's International Building at Fifth Avenue

142

143

Central Park [143] The Bethesda Fountain and Terrace, 1897. John S. Johnston. Architecturally, the area today looks very much like what is seen in this photograph. The human dimension of the scene has been radically altered. Turn-of-the-century proper park behavior was epitomized by the formal clothing, which may explain why the very poor were rarely to be seen in the park, far more than their proximity to the park or the cost of transportation. Blacks of all classes were conspicuous by their absence; they are not to be found in this and most other park photographs of the period, although masses of Blacks lived in the the vicinity of Columbus Circle and today's Lincoln Center, both within easy walking distance of the Fountain.

144

Central Park [144] Bicycling in the Park, 1895 [145] Skating on the Lake with the Dakota in the background, c1888. John S. Johnston

145

146

Columbus Circle
[146] Looking north along Central Park West (then Eighth Avenue) with Broadway to the left. Baseball game is in progress on the site of the present Gulf and Western Building, c1907 [147] Looking east along 59th St, c1925. Edwin Levick

147

148

Museums
[148] The West Side from 73rd St looking north, probably taken from the roof of the Dakota. To the left is Columbus Avenue, with the elevated railroad; to the right, Central Park West and the Park. In the center, the American Museum of Natural History. c1885 [149] Copying the masters in the Metropolitan Museum of Art, c1900

149

150

[150] Construction workers atop the Cathedral Church of St. John the Divine, Amsterdam Avenue at 112th St, looking east, with Central Park at right, c1895

152

Part title illustration (preceding page)
Pedestrians [151] "You are mine, jaywalker," Sign at Fifth Avenue and 42nd St, c1920

Bicycles [152] Bicyclists on the Boulevard (now Broadway) at 78th St, looking north, 1896. Robert L. Bracklow

153

Horses [153] Dousing horses during
hot weather, c1905

154

Elevated lines [154] Third Avenue El in a snowstorm, looking southwest from 55th St with the Chrysler Building at left, 1947 [155] Under the Sixth Avenue El at the corner of 33rd St, looking southwest, 1910

155

Subways [156] Background image: the endpapers of *The New York Subway,* an Interborough Rapid Transit Guide, 1904 [157] Construction workers, probably Italian immigrants, c1904 [158] Kiosks of the 23rd St and Fourth Avenue IRT station, 1905. Detroit Publishing Company [159] The original City Hall IRT station (now closed), 1904 [160] The opening of the New York subway with the president of the Rapid Transit System, Alexander Orr, seated front center, and to his left Mayor McClellan. City Hall station, October 27, 1904

158

159

160

161

[161] For Women Only car of the
Hudson and Manhattan Railroad
Company (also known as the Tube,
and now as the PATH), c1910

162

Automobiles [162] Traffic jam at
Columbus Circle, July 1926

Hindenburg - 1936
Wm. W. Thomas

By Air [163] The Hindenburg above lower Manhattan. Looking northeast from the New Jersey side of the Hudson River, 1936. William Thomas

164

By Ship [164] Charles Lindbergh arriving at the
Battery accompanied by tugboats, yachts, and a
host of other craft, June 2, 1927 [165] The
Normandie in New York, 1938. Alexander Alland,
Sr.

165

(Following two pages)
Bridges [166] Manhattan Bridge, 1936. Berenice
Abbott [167] Manhattan Bridge tower and
roadway, 1911. Irving Underhill

168

[168] Triborough Bridge. In the fore-
ground, Emile Siebern's stainless steel
statue at the Astoria swimming pool,
1938. (Shortly thereafter, the statue
was toppled during a severe storm
and damaged beyond repair.)
Alexander Alland, Sr.

Brooklyn Bridge
[169] The walkway, c1900

170

Brooklyn Bridge [170] Looking
from the Manhattan side, c1900
[171] Print from a waxed-paper
negative, c1925. Jessie Tarbox Beals

171

172

In books of this sort, identifying captions with essential information are necessary (one might say, a necessary evil), but I did take a vow, and on the whole was true to that pledge, not the distract the reader from looking at the photographs by expanding these captions with material readily available in any number of excellent guidebooks, for example those by Paul Goldberger, John Tauranac, and of course the indispensable *AIA Guide to New York City.* A sacred vow.

What better excuse and rationale to violate that pledge than the one-hundredth anniversary of the official opening of the bridge. A salute to that wondrous edifice, to its genius designer John A. Roebling, to his son Washington, who so brilliantly and courageously executed the design, and to his wife Emily Roebling who, when her husband was so tragically crippled by "the bends", taught herself mathematics, steeped herself in the principles and practices of engineering, acted as Washington's liaison, and for almost a decade played a pivotal role in the building of that masterpiece. (An editorial of the day characterized Emily as the "chief engineer of the work".).

To all the Roeblings, to all the engineers, to all the Irish, German, Italian, and other immigrants who risked their lives—some twenty were killed—and to all those who helped bring this bridge about, thanks!

173

Brooklyn Bridge [172] Inspecting
the cables. South St is in background,
1920s [173] Painting the cables,
1940s

**Liberty
Beginning and End**

[174] The Statue of Liberty under
construction in Paris, 1883